Self-Esteem

Embracing Perfection's Absence, Overcoming
Apprehension, And Dispelling Self Uncertainty To Attain
Contentment & Achievement

*(Cease Assuming The Role Of The Victim And Enhance
Your Self-esteem)*

Miguel Stevens

TABLE OF CONTENT

How To Handle Low Self-Esteem 1

Overcoming Shyness 13

How To Encourage Introvert Creativity 33

Strategies For Enhancing Motivation To Achieve Objectives 66

Experimenting With Fairness 73

Recognize And Address Your Self-Esteem Challenges 108

How To Handle Low Self-Esteem 139

A Practice In Positive Thinking 154

How To Handle Low Self-Esteem

Diminished self-worth has a profound and all-encompassing effect on individuals, particularly males. In this society characterized by the presumption of male dominance, the manner in which individuals assess their self-worth can ultimately determine their level of achievement or lack thereof. Each individual, independent of their gender, faces personal challenges when it comes to cultivating confidence and self-esteem. Confidence and self-esteem challenges may be regarded as passing obstacles by some individuals, while others perceive them as formidable hurdles to overcome.

Failing to address one's own subjective perception can lead to adverse consequences in the future. Minor mistakes that go unchecked have the potential to accumulate and manifest as significant challenges that may persist and disturb you in the future. A lack of self-confidence gives rise to elevated levels of stress, heightened anxiety, symptoms of depression, and a pervasive sense of isolation. In its most severe manifestation, it can render you susceptible to substance misuse and other deleterious conduct. It hampers scholastic and vocational excellence and poses a barrier in cultivating meaningful interpersonal connections.

Efficacious Approaches for Nurturing Self-esteem

Regardless of your negative self-perception, it is a reality that this can be altered. The degree may not be significant, however, one's self-perception has the potential to transition from negative to positive, from pessimistic to optimistic. Outlined below are several efficacious techniques to transform your self-perception:

Confront the Internal Voice of Judgment Within You

Please bear in mind that self-esteem is directly linked to one's personal perception. Should there be a person who is overly critical, it would be none other than yourself. There exists within you a facet that consistently imparts the notion of your fallibility. Address this detrimental aspect of your character and question your individual presumptions. This critical self encompasses various aspects, and comprehending their individual manifestations will aid you in approaching them in a constructive manner.

The critic whose judgment is unjustifiable and lacking in empathy. This is your inherent inner essence that consistently fixates on deficiencies and shortcomings. Can you recall if this rings a bell: "I am curious as to why my colleagues applauded during my presentation; I don't think it was as commendable as I personally perceive it to be"? Alternatively, consider this phrase: "How is it conceivable that they failed to recognize the mistake I made during that presentation?"

Rather than engaging in self-criticism and fixating on the negative aspects, adopt a new perspective which acknowledges room for improvement. For instance, consider reframing your thoughts as follows: "While it may not have been flawless, I now have a clearer understanding of areas in which I can enhance my skills" or perhaps "It is truly gratifying to receive recognition for my presentation." I am confident that I have performed satisfactorily."

The unrealistic critic. This represents the intrinsic facet of your being, which perpetually anticipates nothing less than flawless execution, indicating that anything falling below this standard is deemed as a disappointment. At such times, individuals may find themselves uttering the phrase: "This project appeared to be relatively straightforward, why am I unable to execute it successfully?" I'm just plain dumb!"

Rather than being impractical, analyze the experience in terms of its successes and failures. Value your accomplishments and strive to overcome your shortcomings. Perhaps it could be phrased as follows: "Although the outcome may not have been ideal, I am content with the manner in which I structured the content for this presentation." Perhaps I will utilize an alternative format for future instances."

The irrational critic. This represents your tendency to precipitously form conclusions based on superficial observations. She appears to be avoiding direct eye contact with me. She is disinclined to engage in conversation with me. I'm really a loser."

Rather than adopting irrationality and drawing your own conclusions, it is advisable to confront the reality that you perceive. Indeed, she appears to be deliberately evading my presence, albeit the reasons behind her behavior remain veiled in mystery. "I will simply engage with her and inquire." Confronting your perspective directly elevates you above self-indulgence and unfounded despondency. Do not fret if your perception proves to be correct; instead, regard it as a chance to address your weaknesses and refrain from hastily deeming yourself a total failure.

The doomsday critic. At present, you embody your least favorable qualities, assuming the role of a harbinger of misfortune; perceiving minor errors as catastrophic events. Regrettably, my application has been rejected. I shall never attain a state of deserving anything. Nobody will hire me."

Cease! Exercise rationality, for it is merely a solitary instance of failure. While it is undeniable that experiencing rejection can be painful, it is important to recognize that such an occurrence does not imply that you are devoid of any accomplishments or potential for success.

Be Compassionate—to Yourself!

Instead of engaging in self-criticism, it is important to cultivate a sense of self-compassion. You have the capacity to display kindness and empathy towards your friends; it is equally worthwhile to extend the same consideration towards yourself. Your critical self directs its negativity towards another aspect of your character. As you encounter your critical self, it is important to cultivate a sense of compassion towards every facet of your complete persona. This becomes especially significant in challenging circumstances; it is during these moments that self-support becomes imperative. "Presented below are several illustrations of demonstrating self-compassion:

Take the initiative to demonstrate forgiveness for opportunities that have been overlooked. The occurrence of events in this world may not always align with the predetermined intentions that you have formulated. Acknowledging this truth will facilitate your acceptance of the fact that you are fallible. Rather than engaging in criticism, endeavor to console yourself with positive affirmations and words of encouragement, reassuring yourself that circumstances will ultimately resolve favorably.

Respect your being human. We are all susceptible to making errors; it is inherent to our human nature. Acknowledging your inherent fallibility involves recognizing that there are certain tasks in which you may not excel. Rather than admonishing oneself for the error, acquire the ability to transcend it and strive for improvement.

Acquire the skill of controlling your emotions, rather than letting them control you. The presence of emotions distorts our perception of the surrounding world, particularly when it comes to the negative ones. While acknowledging and validating one's emotions carries significance, it is imperative to exercise self-control so that emotions do not overpower one's rationality. In the event that you experience feelings of sadness, isolation, and demoralization, it is advisable to make a record of the personal impact these emotions have on you. Upon overcoming one's emotions, it is advisable to examine the written content, as it is likely to reveal a significant shift in perception when one's emotions no longer exert dominion over them.

Break down your wall of isolation

Individuals with diminished self-esteem tend to seclude themselves as they hold the belief that they lack the requisite worthiness to seek assistance or garner attention. It is imperative to dismantle the barrier that you have erected around yourself in order to foster the growth of your self-esteem. Your perception of yourself has long dictated the course of your life; it is now opportune to open yourself to alternative perspectives on your character as expressed by others. Although it may pose a challenge, there are invariably individuals within your vicinity who are inclined to offer their assistance.

Engage in a sincere and candid dialogue with your acquaintances. Undoubtedly, you possess an individual with whom you share a sense of intimacy and ease. Maintain transparency regarding your emotions and communicate clearly the assistance you require from your closest companions. Occasionally, your companions possess a superior understanding of your predicament compared to your own. To what extent have your companions offered encouragement and assistance during moments of despondency? It is now opportune to lend an ear to the opinions they hold.

The proverbial saying, "like-minded individuals tend to associate with one another," is not applicable in the present circumstances. Avoid the companionship of individuals who will merely indulge in shared lamentation and despondency with you. You are not exhibiting selfish behavior in this situation; rather, you require the company of individuals who possess the capacity to stimulate personal growth and improvement.

Establish contact with individuals of high standing within your social circle. If you are enrolled as a student, it is advisable to engage in a conversation with your professor, guidance counselor, advisor, or coach. These individuals possess extensive expertise in managing the personality-related issues presented by their students over the course of numerous years. If you are a staff member, engage in discussions with your colleagues or your direct superiors. Engage in a conversation with them regarding the difficulties you are encountering in your professional role and convey your requirement for their assistance in overcoming your inhibitions. You will be astounded by the responses people will exhibit when you inquire for their aid. Certain individuals are simply anticipating your initiative in establishing communication with them.

Talk to a professional. It is imperative to consult qualified professionals in psychology or therapy when addressing low self-esteem resulting from deeply ingrained past experiences. Seeking professional assistance is a legitimate course of action.

Overcoming Shyness

Luckily, one can conquer their shyness and lead a fulfilling and industrious existence. Occasionally, we may experience apprehension about engaging in conversation with others due to concerns regarding the possibility of not being liked or reciprocating the liking towards them. Is there any detriment in realizing that you do not establish a harmonious connection with another individual? Suppose that you encounter an individual at a gathering hosted by your closest companion, and subsequent to conversing for a brief duration, you realize that you share no common interests or attributes with this newfound acquaintance, thereby implying that the prospects for establishing a friendship are rather unlikely. That is acceptable. There was no negative impact or offense caused. It is not necessary for you to maintain close friendships with everyone.

Engaging in discourse with individuals who hold similar viewpoints and convictions can be highly fulfilling. Engaging in conversations with individuals who hold contrasting perspectives can be equally beneficial and enlightening. Regrettably, the presence of shyness in an individual acts as a hindrance, impeding their ability to fully perceive and comprehend the abundant opportunities and experiences that exist in the world.

Prior to discussing techniques for overcoming shyness, it is imperative to delve into an analysis of its nature, elucidating its psychological and physiological implications.

Shyness is characterized by a propensity to evade or refrain from engaging with something due to feelings of nervousness, fear, or antipathy.

Are you able to discern a pattern or recurring theme? A deficiency in self-esteem is the root cause of virtually all symptoms experienced by individuals suffering from low confidence.

Shyness exhibits three principal characteristics: Adverse Self-Perception- Social circumstances evoke heightened self-consciousness and concern about others' judgments. You perceive a sense of inadequacy within yourself, where others are perceived as possessing utmost beauty, intelligence, and talent, while you perceive yourself as an intruder.

Excessively preoccupied with deficiencies - You are heavily engrossed in identifying each of your perceived inadequacies to the point where you are unable to recognize the positive aspects of yourself.

Adverse self-dialogue occurs when you veer off topic and extensively highlight all the negative aspects of your being. One begins by considering something as trivial as the perceived mismatch between one's shoes and attire, but eventually proceeds to dismantle their entire appearance or conclude that they lack the aptitude or intelligence to be in the presence of a more accomplished group.

Shyness bears a resemblance to anxiety. If an individual approaches you, it is plausible that you might struggle to articulate coherent thoughts due to the anxiety causing your speech to become disordered and your mental functioning to be impaired. All of these physiological manifestations serve to reinforce your belief in the aforementioned characteristics. Although you may be rendered speechless, your intellect is working tirelessly to highlight each of your disconcerting reactions induced by the unease you are experiencing!

Shyness isn't only about having a sick self-esteem. Although it may initially manifest in such a manner, the condition is sustained by a variety of distinct factors. Throughout the years, you have been recognized as an individual with a tendency towards shyness, and you have come to acknowledge and embrace this characteristic. You do not make any effort to escape the confines of societal expectations, as you have fully embraced that identity. This is impeding your progress.

Have you ever experienced a profound sense of self-satisfaction stemming from accomplishing something remarkable or acquiring a meticulously tailored and aesthetically pleasing ensemble? You are experiencing a heightened sense of euphoria and approach a social gathering with the intention of engaging with others, however, a sudden realization of your innate reserve causes you to hesitate. All of that confidence dissipates, and you find yourself being consigned to the role of a wallflower. Cast off that label and bestow upon yourself a fresh designation. Now is the opportune moment to embrace a mindset of optimism and positivity. You exude self-assurance and possess a genuine enthusiasm for engaging with unfamiliar individuals. Continually practice and affirm until you internalize and persuade your psyche that you are not a passive observer in social situations. You possess a sociable nature and derive pleasure from engaging with and getting acquainted with unfamiliar individuals.

Commitment

It is highly recommended to take proactive actions and carefully determine your objectives regarding

Detach yourself from the mundane aspects of daily life and establish a clear objective. Once you have focused your mind on your desired goal...

One should approach it with utmost conviction and a sense of obligation. When you are organizing and designing

Upon determining your objective, it is imperative to possess unwavering belief in your ability to achieve it, regardless of the challenges that may arise. It is crucial to envision your objective in its entirety, picturing yourself successfully completing whatever endeavor you have embarked upon.

Implement any necessary measures

Once you have made the conscious decision to exert maximum effort and assume the ensuing obligations

The subsequent step involves initiating progress towards attaining your goal, taking actual action.

The most challenging aspect due to the necessity of actively engaging in tasks and truly achieving tangible results.

Contemplating the actions you must undertake is the uncomplicated aspect, as is declaring your unwavering commitment to accomplish them.

Implementing strategies to address the unknown and executing your plan with enthusiasm.

The stage often becomes a stumbling block for many individuals, as fear inhibits our progress.

Sticking with it

As soon as you have committed and embarked upon the pursuit of your aspiration or

In order to actualize your objective, it is imperative to exhibit steadfastness and embrace a willingness to adapt your approach until you attain success.

Ultimately reach your desired goal. Depending on your chosen course of action,

Please allocate sufficient time for this task, as it is imperative that you maintain a high level of focus in overseeing the project.

By starting upon the same foot as before, it has the ability to document the entirety of your undertaking, from commencement to conclusion.

By observing your progress in this manner, you can gain an understanding of the distance you have covered and maintain a focused mindset.

the outcome you aspire to achieve. Life is replete with unexpected idiosyncrasies and has the capacity to unexpectedly hurl any individual into unpredictable circumstances.

Ensure that you persevere and stay resilient in the face of any unexpected challenges, as it is crucial that you continue to propel yourself forward.

The progression perseveres ceaselessly towards your goal. Gradually, apprehension emerges as the primary concern and the primary catalyst leading to the failure of a majority of individuals.

achieve and relinquish their intended objectives, if one were to succumb to apprehension

Persist in continuing to strategically position increasingly larger squares until ultimately they overpower you and you capitulate.

The boundaries are truly limitless if you endeavor with steadfast resolve and tenacity to conquer any obstacles that come your way.

Chapter Five: Cease Engaging in Negative Discourse

The world is already saturated with a sufficient amount of negativity. By adopting a negative demeanor, even toward oneself, one sets an exceedingly unfavorable precedent. Do not ever convince yourself that you are incapable or of little worth. Always exert control over the escalation of negative discourse. Individuals have a tendency to magnify insignificant matters, whereas in reality, they are simply engaging in overthinking and drawing erroneous conclusions by extrapolating minor details. Allow me to illustrate the expediency with which one can alleviate pessimistic thoughts.

Allen engaged in a heated altercation with his spouse. He created a physical separation between himself and her, exited the premises, and forcefully closed the door. Throughout the duration of his stroll in the park, his mind was consumed by thoughts of his anger. He was exacerbating the negativity of the situation. He had made the decision to separate from his spouse.

He grew weary of her incessant complaints. He was clearly preparing to depart and harbored a strong aversion towards her. Indeed, she had simply taken him by surprise and broached a subject for which he was ill-prepared. After enduring a challenging day's work, he was not prepared for the level of discourse she anticipated immediately upon his arrival home. You tend to magnify situations in your thoughts to such an extent that you envision the most unfavorable outcomes. In the case of Allen, while traversing the park, he remained oblivious to any positive aspects. He traversed through the magnificent aspects of nature, yet all that met his gaze was enveloped in an aura of darkness and desolation. As he continued to proceed, he experienced a sudden realization of a child being in a precarious situation. A young individual was on the verge of descending into the waterway situated adjacent to the park. All of his irate musings came to a halt, and his intuition compelled him to proceed with the noble act of rescuing the child. The relevance of this explanation lies in the expeditiousness with which we are able to dismiss thoughts that have a detrimental impact on us. In that fleeting moment, he relinquished all thoughts of his quarrel with his spouse and intervened to rescue the child.

Think of this. By relinquishing an overwhelming thought, you are preventing the inner child from enduring the anguish that accompanies such thoughts. You are succumbing to the forces that are drawing you back into the present moment. Currently, the practice of mindfulness is being widely employed as a means of alleviating stress, wherein individuals can personally engage in this method to escape detrimental thought patterns. In moments of existential uncertainty or self-doubt, it is advisable to engage in the act of inhalation through the nasal passages. Rather than actively entertaining negative thoughts, redirect your focus towards the act of respiration itself. Inhale gradually while counting to seven. Exhale gradually, timing each breath to last for the duration of ten. You are engaging in the process of regulating the oxygen circulation in your body, thereby enabling yourself to achieve a state of tranquility. Individuals who possess a deficit of confidence can employ this effective strategy as a means to eradicate detrimental thoughts aimed at their own being. Rather than expressing an inability to accomplish a task or perceiving it as overwhelming, adopt a mindful approach by taking deep breaths and consciously releasing any pessimistic notions. Engage in this practice when you observe yourself engaging in self-criticism and actively release these critical thoughts, akin to Allen's ability to disengage from distraction. Nonetheless, the degree of distraction you experience will remain within your sphere of control. It facilitates the development of self-assurance and empowers individuals to surpass instances of self-imposed uncertainty.

Consider it from this perspective. Each time you engage in self-deprecating thoughts or make negative remarks about your own abilities, you are reinforcing and perpetuating your dearth of self-assurance. By substituting negativity with a positive action such as focusing on your breath and engaging in conscious breathing, you are effectively preventing your thought processes from overpowering you. This exercise proves to be highly beneficial in alleviating stage fright, preparing for important interviews, and bolstering one's self-assurance during periods of diminished confidence.

Try it now. Inhale through the nasal passages, tallying to seven, followed by an exhalation to the count of ten. The task can be initially challenging due to the ingrained habit of shallow respiration. As you continue to respire, focus your attention back to the present moment. Take notice of all the positive aspects within your surroundings. Employ your faculties of olfaction, gustation, tactility, audition, and so forth. Being fully present in the current moment and relinquishing negative thoughts.

The internal dialogue within your mind is merely superfluous noise. With sufficient practice, you possess remarkable aptitude for relinquishing it, while individuals of self-assurance are skilled at attenuating internal noise and focusing on the present moment. Another factor that contributes to the effectiveness of mindfulness practice is the development of non-judgmental awareness, encompassing the capacity to refrain from evaluating not only external stimuli but also one's own thoughts, emotions, and actions. That implies that in the event of an occurrence, there is no attribution of fault. It is merely an occurrence that takes place. You acquire knowledge from it while not requiring its retention. You effortlessly progress beyond it and subsequently adopt a more composed stance towards life.

Upon mastering the exercises delineated within the book, you will ascertain a notable enhancement in your self-assurance and a heightened ability to exercise self-restraint. Another observation that can be made is that you tend to draw in individuals with greater self-assurance, as a means of replacing those who exploit or negatively impact your own sense of confidence. If individuals exploit your presence, distance yourself from such individuals and cultivate relationships solely with those who contribute positively to your daily existence. Should they fail to do so, it is advisable to allow the burden of the situation to fall upon them, rather than yourself, as you are currently nurturing your self-assurance and no longer require the presence of pessimistic individuals who might undermine it once more.

How To Encourage Introvert Creativity

Introverts possess inherent creativity, a fact that has eluded the majority of individuals. Your aptitude for aggregating and dissecting information proves more advantageous than you may realize. Fundamentally, this is the process through which ingenious concepts are conceptualized and brought into existence, thereby granting introverted individuals a paramount advantage.

In light of this fact, it is imperative for you to continue to cultivate this inherent ability, as it will prove advantageous to you in multiple aspects. Many individuals frequently perceive business as a realm that relies solely on boldness and bravado, yet it is also crucial to possess a significant measure of imagination in order to attain prosperity. The identical perception applies to education. It is widely believed that a high level of intellectual capacity is a prerequisite for advancement in this field. Unbeknownst to them, accomplished individuals utilize their cognitive faculties to foster innovation, rather than solely relying on memorization.

In order to harness the full potential of your introverted mind, it is essential to cultivate habits that can nurture and enhance your creativity. Prior to proceeding, it is imperative that you acknowledge and effectively manage any impediments that may impede your progress in attaining this objective.

Overcoming Creativity Killers

In essence, the principal obstacle to the expression of creativity lies within oneself. While you may possess an understanding of the mechanisms governing your cognitive processes and identifying your areas of growth, cultivating self-confidence necessitates adopting an alternative methodology. This book has the capacity to repeatedly reinforce the brilliance of your introverted mind; however, unless you cultivate a sufficient level of self-trust and faith, its impact will be rendered futile.

Here are three prominent psychological states that you should strive to alter and control in order to unlock and foster your creative potential.

1. Holding the belief that one lacks creativity.

This should not be construed solely within the domain of artistic professions, such as painters, sculptors, musicians, and similar occupations. Each individual possesses a unique form of creativity, which can manifest even through the simplest means of articulation. The manifestation of imagination is necessary for every novel action or contemplation one engages in, and this daily occurrence is evident in various aspects of life, such as interpersonal communication and the anticipation of potential outcomes.

2. Fear of failure.

While it is undoubtedly commendable to recognize and nurture one's creativity, the absence of sufficient courage to actively pursue and manifest these innovative concepts will regrettably render them fruitless endeavors. Numerous individuals abstained from actualizing their conceived notions due to apprehensions of potential failure. It is understandable to experience a certain degree of fear due to the associated implications. Nonetheless, this represents the optimal outcome an individual can anticipate. Failures not only provide valuable insights, but they also serve as indicators of advancement. Consider them as a means to uncover the deficiencies inherent in your strategies or approaches. Identifying deficiencies provides an opportunity to enhance them.

3. Being too judgmental.
Abundant deliberation can stifle ingenuity, as it instills the notion that concepts will be unsuccessful prior to their execution.
Nevertheless, please refrain from misunderstanding this as apprehension towards potential failure. Approaching

situations with excessive judgment almost mirrors a lack of confidence in the potential success of a concept, whereas the alternative implies a lack of self-belief in one's own capacity to achieve success.

Eliminating or managing these obstacles should be your initial step in enhancing your creativity. The subsequent matter that requires your attention is the implementation of suitable protocols.

Cultivating Creativity

A few of the items listed below are inherently present in introverts. Nevertheless, the majority of these behaviors are executed without conscious awareness. Cultivating creativity necessitates the conscious practice of these habits.

1. Continue to seek knowledge.

Data serves as the fundamental building block for the cultivation of creativity. The generation of unique ideas necessitates the existence of preexisting concepts, as previously elucidated, wherein these informational components are deconstructed and reconstituted to acquire fresh insights and forge groundbreaking notions.

Nevertheless, individuals must exercise discernment in their choice of information to assimilate. Consider the case of engaging in continuous television viewing throughout the day. This may be perceived by some individuals as a means to acquire information, and to a certain extent, it can be so. Nevertheless, anticipating the forthcoming occurrences within the context of a preferred reality television program runs counter to its intended purpose.

The most effective approach to acquiring new knowledge entails engaging in active study methods, which may not necessarily entail enrolling in a university setting. Creativity is derived from a synthesis of various elements, including factual knowledge, proficient skills, theoretical principles, and the like. Choosing to acquire proficiency in an alternative language or pursue mastery in playing a musical instrument can prove to be viable alternatives.

Please be mindful that the insights you acquire from this experience extend beyond a singular objective. Your introverted cognition will inherently discern the procedural steps employed to achieve it, and the information it gathers from these steps is indispensable. Put simply, the means serve as the key to enhancing your creativity, such as acquiring the skill to play a piano. There is no need for you to acquire proficiency in it. The essential aspect lies in your comprehension of the mathematical principles which it employs to generate music. Therefore, you may utilize this information in conjunction with other pieces of evidence to generate innovative concepts.

2. Fire up your curiosity.

Continuously strive to attain knowledge about the 'what'. Persist in inquiring and diligently pursuing the explanations regarding the 'why', 'where', 'when', 'who', and 'how'. Your brain resembles a receptacle for currency. The quantity you input is commensurate with the quantity you extract. Put simply, the range or intricacy of your concepts will predominantly hinge upon your depth of knowledge.

Building upon the illustration presented in the preceding narrative, besides scrutinizing the methods employed for acquiring piano skills, there exists a plethora of additional knowledge that can be acquired from this undertaking. What was the reason behind the invention of the piano? How was it conceptualized? Could you provide information regarding its origins, including the specific location and time of origin? Who is the individual responsible for its creation? From what material are the piano strings composed? What were the origins or genesis of notes and chords? - In addition, there are numerous other items/elements/factors.

Please be aware that the differentiating factor between this and the top-ranked option is the additional effort required on your part. This will require research. Fortunately, a wealth of information pertaining to your potential inquiries can be readily accessed through the internet. You are merely required to construct a query, input it into the Google search bar, and peruse the search results.

3. Every idea has its own merit and should be given due consideration, as none should be dismissed outright as foolish or unworthy.

Surprisingly, there exist prosperous commodities in the marketplace that were initially perceived as lacking in intelligence. Please bear in mind that legends are forged through the triumphant accomplishment of seemingly audacious pursuits. An excellent illustration would be the widely recognized Yellow Smiley Face. This renowned emblem has gained global recognition, and due to this seemingly imprudent notion, its originators have now amassed great wealth.

In the future, abstain from dismissing any ideas due to their perceived lack of merit. Engage in exploration and cultivation of the notion, as it could potentially propel you towards triumph.

4. Engage in further reading, actively listen, observe more, and indulge in a wider variety of culinary experiences.

Books, audio recordings, visual works of art, and, indeed, nourishment all stem from the creative faculties of the human mind. Immersing oneself in the presence of these stimuli can engender a heightened state of creativity.

5. Do not anticipate unfavorable responses from others.

In a similar vein as the third point, concepts are often disregarded due to apprehension regarding the perceptions of others. The most adverse outcome they can offer is their subjective perspective, and such evaluations of subjectivity do not substantiate anything beyond the acknowledgment that you can be impacted by them.

Moreover, it is inherently difficult to anticipate the potential reactions of individuals. When examined from an alternative vantage point, these thoughts may be regarded as mere illusions. In order to stimulate your cognitive faculties and foster the generation of novel concepts, it is imperative to exercise restraint and regulate the flow of thoughts, as they have the propensity to confine you to a fixed standpoint.

6. Identify commonalities among disparate entities and ideas.

This mind exercise is quite intricate, yet it offers an assurance of fostering an individual's creative aptitude. In this context, you engage in the process of choosing two distinct items, such as a book and a table. Both items are crafted from timber and fundamentally serve the purpose of containment (books are designed to house knowledge, while the table serves to accommodate miscellaneous objects). After becoming aware of these associations, one proceeds to examine the potential in which tables themselves can communicate information, as well as how books can be employed to bolster other objects.

7. Engage yourself in the splendor of the natural world.

Nature possesses the ability to stimulate the intellect and enhance sensory perception in manners that are beyond the realm of artificial contrivances. It has the capacity to access the depths of our being and inundate us with inspiration, comparable to witnessing the sunset from atop a mountain, where one gazes over a tranquil shoreline, fortifying our morale. The potency of our cognitive faculties bears a direct impact on our capacity for imagination, while emotions possess a transformative quality akin to enchanted powder when applied to it. To put it differently, your inventiveness will markedly excel.

8. Periodically log out from your account.

The advent of smartphones enabled individuals to monitor their email and social media accounts at intervals of approximately fifteen minutes. This situation hinders the nurturing of your creative abilities, as it diverts our focus away from deep reflection. The formation of profound ideas occurs within the depths of our minds, necessitating moments of solitude. The disruption and insistence on instant response by these platforms divert the mind from productive reflection, potentially leading to unrefined and hastily conceived ideas.

By inherent disposition, introverts possess remarkable creative aptitude, and these suggestions serve as supplementary approaches, should they desire to further nurture this characteristic. It is strongly advised, however, that engaging in these habits is essential should you desire to unlock the utmost capabilities of your mind.

3.1 Techniques for Enhancing Your Emotional Intelligence

To engage in advanced critical analysis, it is paramount to possess a comprehensive understanding of oneself. There exist several approaches through which one can effectively structure their thought processes within this domain. An alternative approach is referred to as the VITALS methodology. VITALS is an acronym that represents values, interests, temperament, around-the-clock availability, life mission, and strengths.

Allow us to delve into the subject of utilizing VITALS as a means to comprehensively assess oneself across various domains. The initial segment pertains to the classification of "values." It is imperative to examine your underlying motivations in order to ascertain the alignment of these values with your previous choices. Perhaps you have placed significant importance on your physical well-being and devoted considerable time to maintaining a healthy physique. This holds considerable merit. Another may be family. Have you nurtured a strong connection with your family and established a well-functioning framework of communication and support with them? You might discover that you have attributed excessive importance to certain matters. Perhaps you have dedicated an excessive amount of time to the pursuit of monetary wealth or romantic relationships. This area is strongly aligned with the confluence of motivation. For individuals seeking to maintain motivation and sustain steady progress, it is advisable to consciously recognize one's values and endeavor to prioritize and align them with both professional and personal endeavors.

The subsequent classification is labeled as "interests." This category pertains to values, albeit with some variation. Interests refer to the various endeavors that one finds appealing. This may encompass pastimes, apprehensions, or fervors. Certain individuals may discover that pursuing a career as a professional artist is not feasible for them. However, engaging in the leisurely pursuit of painting as a hobby can contribute to their emotional well-being, overall health, and emotional awareness. Certain individuals are capable of deriving sustenance solely from pursuing their passions. These may encompass a broad spectrum of possibilities. Potential areas of interest may encompass political objectives, activism, or interpersonal connections.

The subsequent classification pertains to "temperament," encapsulating intrinsic inclinations and personal attributes. Would you describe yourself as more introverted or extroverted? In what circumstances do you experience the greatest sense of comfort? This may require an examination of your social connections and their composition. Certain individuals have a predilection for engaging in spontaneous actions. Whilst passing by an unfamiliar restaurant, they might spontaneously opt to give it a chance, as a demonstration. Certain individuals will consistently refrain from engaging in such behavior and will continue to bypass the restaurant unless a prior arrangement is made to visit the establishment.

The letter "A" symbolizes the concept of constant availability, denoting your biological rhythms. Biorhythm is a concept that encompasses the physiological or biological processes that humans must engage in, along with the temporal patterns to which they are inherently linked. Sleep represents an exemplary illustration of a phenomenon characterized by biorhythm. It is an activity that typically commences at a consistent hour each night (if one is fortunate) and ideally concludes at a comparable time each day. Our biorhythms serve as a profound means through which we forge a deep connection with the world. The rotation of the earth exerts a profound influence on our physical beings, and we are inherently enmeshed within the intricate web of its universal cadence. Continuously monitoring records regarding your sexual habits, dietary patterns, physical activity, and other physiological processes. Examining these functions in our lives thoroughly can provide us with a profound understanding of how we structure our lives.

Understanding oneself may initially appear to be a straightforward endeavor. It potentially entails a higher degree of complexity than what is initially perceived. When engaging in introspection and reflecting upon one's decisions, endeavor to identify the aspects of oneself that present vulnerabilities. It is also important to recognize and appreciate your own strengths. Indeed, upon scrutinizing your life, you might discover that you either excessively focus on your strengths or unduly obsess over your weaknesses. Should one be overly preoccupied with their strengths, they may discover a diminished capacity to objectively perceive their weaknesses or areas where they may be less competent relative to others. Individuals who exhibit such a proclivity are inclined towards displaying narcissistic tendencies. They should strive to acquire a greater sense of selflessness. Individuals of this nature possess a positive self-regard, a commendable trait; however, they lack the ability to provide themselves with objective critique concerning areas that warrant improvement in their lives.

The second category of individuals lacks the capacity to perceive and acknowledge their own inherent abilities. They excessively fixate on their shortcomings and internalize self-doubt, questioning their own worthiness or adequacy to receive acknowledgment. They should exhibit a slightly more self-centered attitude. These two categories of individuals personify divergent perspectives on self-centeredness. The suffix "ish" conveys the notion of pertaining to or in a manner characteristic of. Exhibiting selfish tendencies implies self-possession, self-centeredness, and self-governance. This term frequently carries negative connotations, however, it encourages you to consider the word's inherent neutrality. Selfishness denotes a preoccupation with one's own interests and concerns. Certainly, while it is clear that certain individuals should endeavor to display greater selflessness, it is equally important to acknowledge that there exists a significant number of individuals who must strive to cultivate a greater sense of self-interest. These individuals were informed that they were not entitled to anything. These individuals lack the ability to cultivate a suitable level of self-interest and often allow others to take advantage of them. When engaging in the process of self-discovery, it is essential to bear in mind the following. Examine your life for indications of an asymmetry in self-centeredness, in either orientation.

This is a substantial proposition for individuals seeking to enhance their comprehension of non-verbal communication. Acquire a pair of musical instruments that can be utilized jointly with a friend, partner, or colleague. This activity ought to be pursued at a leisurely pace. Invite someone to play along with you and see what you notice. It is advisable to commence by maintaining a steady tempo in order to preserve the timing. However, as one becomes more at ease, they may delve into the groove and venture into experimentation. One can derive significant benefits from establishing a rhythm for others to adhere to and providing them with the necessary support within that rhythm.

Or, another thing that you can do is try playing the guitar or a piano. This can be implemented in a similar manner, utilizing a companion proficient in playing the drums or a percussion instrument. This practice deviates somewhat from the experience of non-verbal communication, as engaging in it by oneself entails conversing with one's own self if there is no practice partner involved. Although that is acceptable, it fails to contribute to the cultivation of a mutually interactive dialogue, thereby resembling more of a solitary practice akin to journaling or pursuing personal artistic endeavors.

Music exemplifies non-verbal communication in its most pristine and unadulterated manifestation. It exhibits a distinct quality in the manner in which it conveys communication via auditory and visual elements, akin to verbal discourse, yet it forgoes the utilization of verbal expressions, save for the incorporation of lyrical composition. The lyrical content represents a nuanced and complex facet of the aesthetic framework encapsulated within this composition. Lyrics are linguistic expressions that, when communicated through singing, have the ability to acquire a profoundly altered significance. Therefore, they are not regarded as verbal communication in the conventional understanding of language.

Nevertheless, the music in question stands as a profoundly enigmatic modality of human expression. Music has the remarkable ability to encapsulate profound emotion, despite being a subtly enigmatic form of artistic expression. Despite considerable practice and years of study, an individual may still not experience noticeable improvement in their musical abilities. This demonstrates the extensive disparities observed among the diverse musical languages existing worldwide. There exist diverse musical languages, encompassing various dialects. Music serves as a profound conduit for communication and self-expression, capable of conveying both banal and profound messages that reflect the depths of our inner being.

Music is comprised of frequencies, which consist of measurements of the oscillations of sound waves resulting from various phenomena. Sound serves as a profound medium for connecting individuals, and it is widely recognized that music possesses the capacity to evoke profound and distant recollections in individuals afflicted with Alzheimer's or dementia. This is due to the profound interrelation between music and our perception of the world, as sound accompanies every single one of our experiences. Therefore, the significance of sound becomes equally paramount to that of taste, sight, touch, and smell. It serves as a fundamental means by which we maintain connectivity with the global community. Music frequently incorporates a visual element, particularly when one is observing a live performance; the auditory aspect serves as the integral link to one's emotions and sentiments.

If one were to attend a symphony orchestra performance and inquire of each member of the audience about their respective experiences at its culmination, it is highly likely that variances in responses would be observed. Certain individuals may contend that it possessed exceptional aesthetic appeal and evoked a profound sense of captivation due to the orchestra's extraordinary prowess. Certain individuals may express that they perceived the composition as being sorrowful and experienced moments of melancholy while witnessing it. Some individuals may assert that the impact on them was minimal and they were not particularly interested in the performance. An individual lacking a response may resort to fabrication.

This showcases the profound capacity of music to elicit experiences for individuals and the remarkable potential that music possesses to evoke emotions and stimulate thoughts within each of us. This is non-verbal communication.

In addition, it may be noted that verbal communication also exhibits a similar inconsistency. In the context of an oral discourse, if you were to inquire of the comparable audience subsequent to a public address or instructional session, the responses obtained would likely exhibit similar levels of detachment. Certain individuals are inclined to provide a precise synopsis of the key elements, while others may lack the ability to elucidate the sequence of events. Certain individuals may proffer their personal assessment of the oratory rather than focusing on the substantive aspects. The perception of content, whether conveyed through spoken or non-spoken means, cannot be easily quantified or predicted.

Growth

Apprehension can impede one's personal and professional development. The pursuit of personal growth is a crucial aspect of human development, contributing significantly to our engagement and enthusiasm towards life. As individuals age, it is natural for personal development and transformation to occur. However, the progress towards maturation and self-improvement can be impeded by the presence of fear. Consider the option of frequenting a fitness center and engaging in resistance training. As your training duration increases, your muscles will experience enhanced strength due to their ability to adapt to heavier weights. As your muscular strength improves over time, you will progressively augment the weights you lift. Our cognitive faculties function in a similar manner to our physical musculature. If we challenge ourselves by exposing ourselves to new situations or experiences, our minds will expand, so to speak. While this process unfolds, we can continue to subject ourselves to novel circumstances, nurturing the growth of our comfort zone in tandem with the expansion of our cognitive faculties. The objects and concepts we perceive as novel and intimidating will undergo a transformation, as our perception of safety and comfort expands to encompass a wider range of them, including those that were once unfamiliar and anxiety-inducing.

Fear engenders a disposition towards negativity or pessimism.

When encountering fear, our attention is fixated on anticipated perils rather than the potential benefits that may arise from the source evoking fear. Therefore, fear engenders pessimism rather than optimism. Pessimism impedes progress as it hinders our ability to approach potential situations with a mindset focused on the potential benefits that may arise. Instead, it forces us to perceive these situations through a lens solely focused on the possible negative outcomes. What potential factors might pose a risk or endanger my well-being? What are all the potential drawbacks that could arise from this situation? When endeavoring to enhance one's self-esteem, it is crucial to foster a sense of optimism. Elevated self-regard emanates from a favorable perspective, whereas diminished self-regard emanates from an unfavorable perspective. In the pursuit of enhancing one's low self-esteem, it is essential to direct our attention towards positive aspects and cultivate a sense of optimism. However, the presence of fear impedes our ability to undertake this constructive endeavor.

Fear Inhibits Cognitive Functioning

Within this section, you shall encounter the phenomenon that instills apprehension in us, denoted as "the stimulus." The stimulus may encompass a broad range of occurrences, spanning from encountering an enraged bear to receiving an invitation to a social gathering, or even encountering an ex-partner who wishes to engage in conversation. This term serves as a comprehensive designation for the underlying cause of our anguish.

Fear inhibits the cognitive processing of stimuli, as the primal fight or flight mechanism in the brain is designed to elicit rapid responses that surpass the cognitive abilities of our conscious mind. During the era of our primitive ancestors, had we occupied ourselves with the intricate task of evaluating the bear situated in our vicinity and deliberating upon our subsequent course of action, it is certain that we would have succumbed to its predatory instincts prior to reaching a conclusion. Hence, fear inhibits cognitive processing of the stimulus. However, in our present era, this can prove to be more of a drawback than an advantage. Fear inhibits the capacity for the conscious processing of stimuli, preventing one from engaging in cognitive operations such as logical reasoning grounded in factual evidence and the careful evaluation of advantages and disadvantages. In the event of permitting this occurrence, it is conceivable that we could assess the stimulus as lacking any harm to our well-being and though apprehensive, proceed with our intended course of action. Frequently, this would probably be the scenario, however, to determine this, it is necessary to initially analyze the stimulus. The issue lies in the fact that once gripped by fear, it becomes exceedingly difficult to extricate oneself from this state and initiate the rational processing of the situation. We will explore several approaches to accomplish this objective in subsequent sections of this chapter.

Compromise is not a constituent of fear

An admirable characteristic of individuals is our capacity to engage in compromises. If we discern a quantity to be excessive or inadequate, we can reach a consensus that is in close proximity to our preferred threshold, while refraining from outright rejection. When one experiences a fear response, it manifests as either an affirmation or a negation, devoid of potential concessions due to the agitated state that fear induces. If one were to carefully contemplate whether a situation is overwhelming, it is possible to arrive at the conclusion of settling for a middle ground or a similar alternative. For instance, drawing upon the aforementioned example, if you receive an invitation to visit a bar in an unfamiliar locality, accompanied by individuals you have not met before, it is plausible that you might immediately encounter a sense of apprehension upon being asked, subsequently followed by a compulsion to supply a response in the affirmative or negative. Had the fear not overwhelmed you, you could have potentially reached the conclusion that you are receptive to socializing with these unfamiliar individuals. However, embarking on an outing to a new neighborhood with them all at once may appear overwhelming. Consequently, it would have been appropriate to express your willingness to accompany them for a single drink in a locale near your residence before returning home, while permitting them to proceed to the new neighborhood, or arrive at some equivalent compromise of this nature.

Strategies For Enhancing Motivation To Achieve Objectives

Motivation denotes an act of propulsion instigated by logic or intention. It is crucial to comprehend this significant aspect: the presence of a reason and purpose will engage and stimulate motivation.

An illustration of this would be the difficulty in progressing towards a goal when there is a lack of discernible rationale or objective. To clarify, in order to initiate progress and propel yourself forward from your current situation, it is necessary to possess a clear motive or rationale for exerting the necessary effort.

If you possess a strong desire to accomplish a certain task, you will likely experience a higher level of motivation. You will feel compelled to take action without having to exert conscious effort, as the desire will drive your actions. It is important to bear in mind that there may exist valid motivations or objectives that lead to a lack of motivation, resulting in a state of inertia.

Certain individuals define motivation as a compelling force or a deep-seated yearning. Alternative definitions of motivation encompass the professional endeavors undertaken by individuals. For me, motivation holds no significance. Motivation is essentially the underlying force that fuels one's drive, passion, and efforts. This "energy" has an impact on the level of motivation, an individual's motives, and the resultant dynamic of action and outcomes that arise from motivation.

Furthermore, this energy known as motivation arises from the extent to which an individual is living a purpose-driven life and the extent to which one is in harmony with their authentic self, their innermost being.

From my perspective, motivation can be defined as a force encompassing physical, psychic, emotional, and spiritual energies. This energy may be characterized, on one extreme of a spectrum, as positive, vibrant, robust, dynamic, exploratory, exhilarating, spirited, therapeutic, etc., while on the other end it can be described as stagnant, impeded, lifeless, inert, despondent, unfavorable, destructive, etc.

Motivation is a psychophysical phenomenon, primarily centered around bodily factors. Based on my observations, few individuals express their motivation by saying "I think I'm motivated." Instead, it is more common to hear phrases such as "I feel motivated" or, conversely, "I don't feel very motivated."

Furthermore, the phrases "fire in the belly", "lack of enthusiasm", "instinctual decision", and "physical weakness despite mental willingness", among numerous other expressions that revolve around the abdominal region, also indicate the body as the primary source of motivation (as opposed to the mind), the core of this energy that propels individuals into action and sustains their state of motivation.

Motivation, in my perspective, can be described as a palpable sensation.

Therefore, in my perspective, each person possesses motivation, albeit it may not align with another individual's preference or even the manner in which we personally would select.

So,

When I engage in internet browsing, instead of concentrating on the task at hand, I am driven to do so.

When I opt to perceive employees as functions rather than individuals, I am driven by motivation.

I am driven to engage in gossip, bullying, and sarcasm in my speech instead of communicating respectfully, lovingly, and compassionately.

When I opt to compromise my business practices and principles by succumbing to greed, instead of adhering to a moral framework, I am compelled.

I am motivated when I opt to perceive conflict and negotiation as a win-lose situation rather than a win-win scenario.

I am driven when I opt to engage in tax evasion and deviate from my dietary restrictions.

When I opt to allocate only 75% of my energy and commitment to my work instead of giving my full effort, I am propelled by motivation.

I am driven when I opt for dishonesty, deceit, and theft over adhering to principles of honesty, integrity, and trust.

When I opt for behaving in an immature manner instead of demonstrating emotional intelligence, I am driven.

When I succumb to the influence of my ego and partake in counterproductive actions, rather than operating from my genuine and sincere self, I am driven.

When I opt to suppress my emotions and passively engage with the television, as opposed to wholeheartedly immersing myself in my obligations, I am driven by my inner determination.

When I opt for engaging in an extramarital relationship instead of investing effort in improving my intimate partnership, I am driven by motivation.

When I opt for antipathy, rather than affection, I am driven.

So, everyone is motivated.

Once more, to me, the essence resides in the inherent excellence of the driving force, and further still, in the underlying foundation beneath the quality of that force.

The factor that influences the caliber of the energy referred to as motivation, in my view, is purpose.

For me, purpose is driven by the heart rather than being driven by mental and ego-driven motivations. The essence of our existence derives its significance from the purpose it holds. Once again, from my perspective, motivation is intricately connected to purpose and significance.

The distinction between purpose driven by the heart and purpose driven by the ego is what determines individuals' literal and figurative location in the spectrum between having a purpose and being purposeless, and finding meaning and experiencing meaninglessness in one's professional, personal, and recreational endeavors.

In many aspects of life, we transition from undertaking an action to achieving a corresponding outcome, repeatedly moving from action to result. The query at hand pertains to the factors that motivate and determine my behaviors. What is the underlying force that fuels the motivation and energy behind my actions? The trajectory of an individual's life is frequently assessed based on this inherent progression, and many also evaluate "success" in accordance with this transition from action to outcome.

In the grand scheme of things, for me personally, the vitality and caliber of the cause-and-effect dynamic and the vigor and caliber with which one associates with 'achievement' is correlated to whether one is leading a life 'with intention' and from where one's intention originates (either from the ego or from the heart).

Experimenting With Fairness

Have you ever observed your surroundings and pondered over the existence of socio-economic disparities between the privileged individuals and those who are disadvantaged? It is possible that you may have experienced a slight tinge of jealousy towards individuals who possess the ability to effortlessly articulate their thoughts and emotions, whereas your own self-assurance has hindered your own proficiency in doing so. A study conducted by an Italian individual named Pareto resulted in the formulation of the 80/20 rule. The statement suggests that although the majority, or 80 percent, of individuals in a specific region of Italy exhibit diligent labor, it is the minority, or 20 percent, who accrue the majority of the advantages. The intriguing aspect of this premise lies not in its material applications to the privileged and underprivileged individuals. This principle is applicable to all facets of existence. Inequities exist in life, causing numerous individuals to forego the enjoyments that life can offer, primarily owing to their inability to effectively incorporate this principle into their own lives. Allow me to demonstrate the positive impact this can have on your self-assurance.

Please document your areas of proficiency.

It is possible that you perceive this as insignificant, however, it holds considerable significance. You possess the knowledge and skills necessary to carry out domestic tasks. You possess the knowledge and ability to take care of your personal well-being, including the practice of oral hygiene. Perhaps you possess the ability to operate an automobile. We kindly request your scrutiny of all the proficiencies you possess. Now, it is imperative to examine the proportion of your lifetime allocated to engagements that impart unease and a sense of inadequacy in you. These are occasions wherein individuals engage in activities that do not bring about feelings of happiness or satisfaction, but are merely endured due to societal expectations or personal obligations. In order to enhance your self-esteem, it is necessary to allocate a greater proportion of your time toward fostering positive thoughts and feelings about yourself. Consequently, it is imperative that you prioritize engaging in activities where you possess inherent capabilities, rather than investing time and effort in pursuits where you lack proficiency.

Let us assume that you allocate a substantial portion, specifically 20 percent, of your time engaging in activities that do not contribute to the enhancement of your self-esteem. Thus, you need to increase the amount of time you spend doing things that please you and make you feel like you have something positive to offer life. I would propose that you allocate additional time towards engaging in the following activities. By dedicating more time to activities that enhance your self-confidence, you will discover a corresponding increase in the duration of your positive self-perception. If you are able to consistently increase that percentage on a daily basis, while maintaining a written record of the actions you undertake to enhance that percentage, you will observe a gradual reduction in detrimental self-perceptions.

Engaging in the pursuit of knowledge through reading and finding entertainment in educational documentaries on television leads to the acquisition of knowledge and enlightenment.

Engaging in crossword puzzles - thereby enhancing your vocabulary proficiency.

Engaging in cognitive exercises such as Luminosity to enhance the agility of your brain.

Devoting additional time to self-care and personal growth.

Spending additional time with individuals who exude positivity can contribute to the development of self-assurance.

Engaging in extended periods of culinary experimentation can be highly fulfilling and offers the opportunity for communal enjoyment with companions.

Devoting additional time to assisting loved ones or individuals in need invariably enhances one's self-perception by fostering a greater sense of positivity.

Indeed, as one becomes cognizant of the influence that one's perspective has on the outcomes of life, one also realizes that they possess a greater degree of control over their own life than initially anticipated. Moreover, this will also enhance your self-assurance. It is essential to make progress in one's life, and at times, it can be advantageous to establish achievable objectives that bring personal satisfaction on a daily basis. Record them and ensure that they are activities that foster a sense of self-empowerment. By adopting this approach, you shift the probabilities in your favor and are afforded the opportunity to derive significantly more satisfaction from life, alleviating any persistent self-doubt regarding one's worthiness. You are indeed capable and it is imperative that you disengage from any idle moments you may have been using to dwell in unhappiness and inhibit your self-expression. By making conscious decisions regarding your personal growth and engaging in activities aimed at enhancing your capabilities, you are actively opting for a positive course of action that can significantly augment your likelihood of attaining happiness.

A recurring shortcoming of mine has been the neglect of allocating personal time to myself. I engage in this practice consistently as I firmly believe that equitable allocation of time for personal growth and the pursuit of happiness is essential for all individuals. Upon documenting these percentages and viewing them in a stark presentation, one abruptly apprehends that a substantial 80 percent of their time is devoted to unfavorable pursuits, with a glaring inadequacy in attending to activities that foster a positive self-perception. This pertains to the exploration of one's personal identity. Do not base your self-worth on the opinions of others and cultivate self-compassion by refraining from self-judgment. Life should not be defined by judgments, however, unfairness arises when one succumbs to insecurity rather than embracing life wholeheartedly in every endeavor. Produce a visual representation of the balance, depicting the factors that contribute positively or negatively to your self-esteem. By carefully placing the aspects that elicit contentment and those that induce feelings of insecurity or inadequacy, it is highly probable that the weight of concerns will surpass that of positive attributes. It is incumbent upon you to maintain equilibrium and transition towards a profoundly optimistic perspective on life and its treatment. There exist constructive actions one can undertake, and it is imperative to acknowledge that if one lacks proficiency in a particular task, it may indicate a lack of suitability and warrant exploration of alternative pursuits, or alternatively necessitate additional dedication to honing the skill through practice. As you become more acquainted with that specific activity, your confidence increases and you experience greater ease in performing it.

List of Tasks for Your Attention

The sense of satisfaction derived from fulfilling tasks on your daily agenda is indeed gratifying, however, it is imperative not to allow the quantity of checked items or the absence thereof to dictate your self-worth.

Morin asserts that basing your self-worth on your achievements is analogous to constructing a house on an unstable foundation, even though experiencing satisfaction with your accomplishments is a common inclination. In order to experience genuine self-satisfaction, one must consistently strive for achievement, thereby potentially avoiding activities that entail the risk of failure.

Your Job

Irrespective of the nature of your vocation or your personal sentiments towards it, your occupation does not inherently define your individuality.

Your Social Media Audience

Consider a hypothetical situation in which you lack a million followers on Instagram or receive minimal retweets on Twitter. In the realm of our digitalized society, it may indeed seem as if one's value is contingent upon a numerical representation. However, it is crucial to recognize that the essence of an individual surpasses the limitations of mere data visible on a display.

Your Age

Regarding numerical values, your age merely consists of numerical digits. Certain individuals may express that you are either excessively youthful or excessively old, nonetheless, it is crucial to comprehend that this is precisely the characteristic of your current identity. Therefore, it would be advisable to simply embrace and embody your genuine self.

Your Appearance

If it is necessary to alter your appearance, do so for your own personal benefit. However, it is essential to understand that your worth should not be defined by your outward appearance. "A picturesque physique or an alluring countenance will not endure indefinitely," Morin writes. The condition of having a receding hairline, a face marked by wrinkles, and being at a certain stage in life that is associated with a period of personal turmoil can be distressing for individuals who attribute their sense of value to their outer attractiveness.

Other People

I am accountable for comparing my abilities and achievements with those of individuals of the same profession and age as mine. However, it has come to my realization that it is crucial for me to adhere to a direct and uncompromising approach in embarking on my personal journey—and the same applies to you.

Embrace and pursue your personal journey.

You do you. Provide them with an opportunity to pursue their endeavors. Occasionally, it is acceptable for individuals to surpass you on the journey of life. We are each progressing at varying rates.

The Extent of Your Running Capacity

Have you ever experienced the occurrence of setting a personal goal to successfully complete a mile-long run, and subsequently engaging in self-criticism and disappointment if you were unable to achieve it? It is a common event, but please acknowledge that your worth is derived from making a sincere effort, rather than the speed at which you accomplish your goal.

Your Grades

Perhaps examinations cause you distress or the academic demands of school are inherently challenging. Academic performance does not solely determine one's intellectual acumen, nor does it accurately measure qualities such as dedication and reliability.

The quantity of companions in your social circle.

The greater the number of companions, the more joyful the occasion becomes. At times. Nevertheless, irrespective of whether one possesses a multitude of acquaintances or a limited circle, the determining factor lies in the manner in which individuals interact and their willingness to provide support during times of adversity.

Your current marital or partnership status

Unattached and open to new connections. It does not imply that you are unworthy of love or admiration—it signifies that you are prioritizing self-care and nurturing your own well-being.

Possessing Wealth or Experiencing Financial Deprivation

Irrespective of whether you possess great wealth or have limited financial resources, the amount of money you possess or earn does not determine your intrinsic worth. Morin articulates that the strategy of incurring debt to feign a sense of wealth ultimately fails, as material possessions and business endeavors possess financial value but do not reflect one's personal worth.

Your Likes

I am refraining from engaging in a conversation about Facebook likes; rather, I am interested in delving into your personal preferences, such as your musical tastes or film selections. Indulge in your personal preferences, irrespective of whether they align with the realms of "superior craftsmanship" or "lesser artistic value."

Anything or anyone other than yourself.

Main focus: The determination of your worth rests entirely on your own actions and choices. You display commendable behavior by declaring your commendability based on objective evidence, rather than relying on mere self-assurance. Engage in introspection and have faith in your own competence.

Self-Assessment of My Personal Value

Joy was a quantifiable measure, accompanied by a delightful ensemble, and commanding the utmost admiration from every individual I encountered.

As one might reasonably surmise, this mentality had severely detrimental effects. I lacked the capability to engage with the factors that brought me satisfaction. This led to an exceptionally isolated period in my life, during which I ended up losing most of the acquaintances I had believed to have accumulated over the years. I found myself alone, and gave no consideration to my true identity.

After extensive periods of introspection and self-care, I strive to live consistently as an individual deserving of love. I ultimately commenced establishing personal standards for gratification, over which I held complete autonomy. The endorsement, acknowledgment, or applause of others will bear no influence on my life unless I hold the same perception of myself. I am not going to rouse or arouse another individual in the near future, thus I must focus on maximizing my personal growth and development.

Every day represents an opportunity for experiential learning. I am of the opinion that it is unlikely for anyone to wake up feeling their optimal state. However, at the commencement of my journey, I made a personal commitment to consistently demonstrate utmost care, respect, and affection towards myself, akin to how I would treat an individual whom I hold in high esteem. Currently, I hold a high regard for the person that I have become.

Before delving further into this topic, it is imperative to elucidate the distinction between narcissism and self-assurance, thereby assuaging any guilt you might harbor for prioritizing your own well-being. Narcissism entails the recognition and admiration of one's own attributes, consequently fostering an excessive, self-centered disposition. It is not enough for narcissistic individuals to have self-admiration; they feel compelled to publicly assert their self-regard, believing it elevates their self-worth above that of anyone else. Despite the lack of outward indication, I maintain the belief that this mental state is influenced by the viewpoints of others.

They ought to recognize that you perceive yourself as unparalleled.

Self-confidence is characterized by a positive self-perception. You appreciate the positive attributes you possess, while also acknowledging the areas where you may be more susceptible or vulnerable. These characteristics do not cause you to experience humiliation, nor do you subject yourself to self-deprecation due to their presence. You acknowledge and embrace the emotions that come with having imperfections, and make a concerted effort to strengthen and improve yourself. Self-assurance provides you with a feeling of comfort, rather than superiority. You fervently embrace favorable circumstances but remain resolute in the face of adverse moments.

Regardless of the challenges you may encounter, you have adopted the mindset that you will consistently rely on your own capabilities to navigate through them. The aforementioned fact is the foundation for the "assurance" that enables the concept of "self."

What is the rationale underlying my decisions?

What I have come to discern through the process of self-discovery is that engaging in such activities does not render one captivating. Moreover, it proves difficult for someone to gravitate towards an individual who exhibits no discernible personal inclinations. The ancient tradition of mine diminished the distinctiveness inherent in my character and hindered my recognition of the extraordinary nature of having particular interests.

As I continue to grow and evolve as an individual, while recognizing my unique qualities and abilities, I consistently question the motivations behind my pursuits and endeavors. Will this better me? Is my reluctance to engage in this task based on genuine personal preference, or is it rooted in a fear of failure? Am I considering myself unworthy of participating in this and therefore choosing not to take part? Do I possess a genuine potential for deriving enjoyment from developing an affinity towards this particular subject matter?

As previously stated, I am actively striving towards becoming the person I aspire to be. Just because I have achieved remarkable progress since my high school days does not imply that it is challenging to revert back to the former mindset due to apprehension. By consistently engaging in self-reflection, I ensure that the decisions I make are based on my own personal values and priorities, rather than being influenced by the opinions or perceptions of others.

I attribute my self-esteem to the process of making informed decisions and recognizing that I am suited for making such choices.

Opinions of Other Individuals" or "Perspectives from Other Individuals

Therefore, I have discussed my personal encounter. However, I am not by myself in this endeavor, thus prompting me to write this book. Therefore, this is why I engage in speaking, mentoring, and coaching as well. As we extend our generosity to others, we experience enhanced personal well-being and a heightened sense of fulfillment. I am aware that countless individuals face challenges relating to self-esteem and confidence. Through my extensive research, personal conversations, and experiences in coaching, I have compiled a comprehensive list of common struggles and recurring patterns in self-esteem. It is imperative to note that a few of these struggles resonated with my own personal journey as well. I have not presented an extensive array of statistics; rather, I have offered observations based on my findings.

There is an inadequate presence of self-esteem resources tailored to men on social media platforms.

When one evaluates the self-esteem-related content shared on various social media platforms, an observation can be made that the majority of individuals contributing to this discourse are women.

It is commendable that women are embracing a candid and assertive dialogue regarding self-esteem, and I extend my gratitude to any woman who embarks on reading this book for self-improvement. Nonetheless, I do hold apprehensions about society perceiving male vulnerability as a sign of weakness, resulting in its suppression. I harbored similar concerns. I was genuinely apprehensive about the potential impact of displaying vulnerability, as it could potentially diminish the favorability of my reception by a female counterpart. Nonetheless, paradoxically, I have observed that embracing my true self with greater transparency has attracted significantly heightened levels of support from individuals well-suited for such rapport. It does not entail daily complaints on my part (as I generally feel splendid most days); rather, it pertains to occasional instances when I encounter a challenge or have a noteworthy experience that I choose to divulge. It highlights the aspect of my humanity and dispels the misconception that I am an emotionless automaton operating ceaselessly.

I would like to express my gratitude, nevertheless, to the individuals who engage in writing and exchanging their thoughts. It\'s an amazing ability. For those who do not share this perspective, I completely acknowledge and highly regard every individual reader. My sincere hope is that by the conclusion, I may assist in fostering a greater willingness to be more receptive.

There is an increased discourse concerning confidence.

There exists a nuanced distinction between self-esteem and confidence, however, they are interconnected as previously discussed. However, there is further information to be elaborated upon regarding confidence. When an individual endeavors to enhance their self-assurance in a particular skill or domain, yet continues to experience a lack of profound self-satisfaction, I opine, based on personal experience, that this may be attributed to the negligence of self-esteem or the necessity for introspective self-acceptance. Like I did. I am interested in examining the concept of self-esteem. Self-esteem permeates every aspect of an individual's life, which is why we have chosen to collectively emphasize its significance in this publication.

Body image

This is not a matter that I have personally encountered to a significant extent. Indeed, during my earlier years, I possessed a slightly more substantial physique and was prone to skin blemishes; however, as I matured, I managed to attain a commendable level of physical fitness and overall well-being.

This is a domain in which women encounter difficulties, due to the perpetual pursuit of flawlessness perpetuated by these models who are provided with an abundance of embellishing cosmetics, favorable lighting, and the like. Men suffer too though. The images portraying individuals with well-defined abdominal muscles, prominent facial structures, and flawless complexion prove to be unhelpful.

I am aware that individuals may experience discomfort or dissatisfaction with aspects of their physical appearance, such as their height, weight, complexion, and overall aesthetics.

There are certain aspects that are within our control and others that are beyond our influence.

I desire individuals to feel at ease in their natural state. I must admit that my level of expertise in this matter is limited, but I have recently recollected a relevant piece of information. During the period spanning from my late teens to early twenties, I diligently pursued the goal of attaining a well-defined abdominal musculature. Comparison was a killer. I performed with satisfactory proficiency at certain junctures, yet during times of subpar performance, I experienced a deep sense of dissatisfaction and compelled myself to strive harder, disapproving of the reflection in the mirror. I was not in poor condition, simply not in an immaculate state. Contrary to popular belief, the concept of perfection is nonexistent. Subsequently, I will be addressing the topic of body image.

External validation

This has been an immensely debilitating experience that has inflicted lasting harm upon me over the course of numerous years. I have not entirely moved on from it, however, I have greatly developed a stronger capacity for self-love than I previously possessed. Individuals constantly seek validation from various sources, including their superiors at their workplace, companions, romantic partners, relatives, and increasingly, digital platforms such as social media, in the contemporary era. The inclination to appease others originated during my youthful years, as I desired to ensure the well-being and contentment of both my immediate surroundings and my family, particularly during the unfortunate event of my brother's passing.

This trend has significantly deteriorated over the course of the past decade, primarily due to the prevalence of social media. Individuals consistently seek dopamine stimulation through text messages and various forms of social media. We also address the matter of taking concrete steps.

Comparisons

This bears some resemblance to its predecessor, albeit with distinct variations. Due to the ubiquity of social media and media platforms, we are perpetually engaging in self-comparisons. I simply need to peruse social media platforms to observe the most recent author unveiling their book, garnering a multitude of followers or enthusiasts on YouTube. Previously, my habitual practice involved incessantly scrutinizing outcomes and feeling disheartened by their failure to surpass those achieved by individuals at the pinnacle.

It is advisable to observe individuals such as Tony Robbins, Gabby Bernstein, and Rob Dial (whom I greatly admire), but refraining from comparing oneself to them is crucial. Engaging in such comparisons can have detrimental effects on one's well-being.

Loneliness

The lack of companionship is an extremely distressing situation. I am frequently encountering numerous posts that predominantly revolve around feelings of solitude, which deeply sadden me. I am able to perceive my adolescent self, experiencing profound solitude while grappling with the uncertainty of how to establish meaningful friendships.

It appears that individuals display reluctance or lack the knowledge to proactively initiate communication with others.

I am determined to bring this to a conclusion.

Assurance in particular matters

I observe that numerous individuals express a deficiency in their confidence levels. This appears to exhibit a prevailing pattern of social confidence or dating confidence. Allow me to state that I have experienced both of these matters firsthand. Additionally, it is worth noting that confidence can be likened to a muscle, but in order to develop confidence, it is essential to actively engage in actions, after which a sense of confidence will gradually emerge. I will delve into strategies for building confidence in later chapters of this book. I assert that fostering a sense of self-worth will yield a favorable ripple effect on an individual's level of assurance.

Recognize And Address Your Self-Esteem Challenges

A plethora of challenges stem from a lack of adequate self-esteem. With which ones do you encounter difficulties, and can you explain the reasons behind those challenges? What strategies can be implemented to address these challenges with the aim of enhancing one's current quality of life? This represents the initial stride among our comprehensive set of seven steps aimed at promptly elevating one's sense of self-worth.

First Step: Confronting the Consequences Resulting from Low Self-Esteem

Relationship Issues

For individuals possessing a strong sense of self-worth and contentment within themselves, establishing long-lasting relationships or entering into matrimony provides a conducive environment wherein one can discover love, validation, and during challenging circumstances, unwavering assistance. Individuals with diminished self-confidence experience significant and detrimental effects on their relationships as a result of these emotions.

Scholars are discovering that self-esteem not only influences one's self-perception but also detrimentally affects their expectations regarding partners and relationships. It prompts one to rely solely on their partner for affirmation and acceptance. The presence of personal insecurities renders a relationship incapable of offering the fundamental qualities that are characteristic of a wholesome and prosperous relationship dynamics.

In instances of unfavorable circumstances, individuals with diminished self-worth anticipate not assistance, but rather the contrary from their significant others. They anticipate that their significant other will experience disappointment in them and cease to harbor love for them.

Jealousy

Envy and diminished self-worth are closely intertwined with the aforementioned interpersonal challenges. One can surmount feelings of envy and elevate self-worth; however, this process requires a considerable amount of time and effort. It takes reflection. It requires effort, nevertheless it is achievable.

The peril of jealousy stemming from a lack of self-esteem resides in its potential to profoundly impact an individual's cognitive function, as evidenced by research indicating parallels with the neurological responses observed in instances of shock or bereavement. The potent nature of the combination of jealousy and low self-esteem is decidedly detrimental.

Due to the profound lack of self-esteem you possess, it is likely that you will persistently perceive your partner as potentially receptive to the advances of others, as you believe yourself to be undeserving of love. These sentiments render you susceptible to harboring bitter envy at any given moment. Overcoming jealousy necessitates substantial support and personal resolve, yet it is an achievable feat.

Depression/Anxiety/Panic Attacks

This particular issue of low self-esteem is the utmost perilous. Depression, anxiety, and panic attacks are formidable challenges to both one's self-esteem and mental well-being, carrying significant ramifications.

Depression

There exists a robust association between depression and self-esteem in relation to the shared perception of worthlessness. Subsequently, when low self-esteem precipitates depression, the impact is twofold. This cognitive process is commonly induced by depression, while a similar outcome can be attributed to diminished self-worth.

Individuals who struggle with diminished self-esteem may find themselves ensnared within a sequence of negative cognitive patterns, characterized by perceiving oneself as lacking value, viewing the external world as untrustworthy and hostile, and harboring pessimistic apprehensions regarding future prospects.

Anxiety and Panic Attacks

The correlation between anxiety and panic disorders exhibits a more nuanced nature compared to its association with depression, yet its impacts can be equally destructive. A lack of self-confidence leads individuals to question each decision, subsequently resulting in heightened anxiety and an increased susceptibility to panic attacks. Due to the individual's diminished self-confidence and persistent feelings of inadequacy coupled with a perceived inability to handle any kind of challenge, their capacity to arrive at sound judgments remains compromised.

Additionally, the experience of anxiety and panic can give rise to phobias, thereby further constraining one's lifestyle. Individuals who possess diminished self-esteem tend to lack the necessary confidence to effectively address such types of challenges. They will hold the belief that it is unattainable for them to accomplish such a feat.

Action Plan

Low self-esteem can give rise to a diverse range of issues related to interpersonal relationships, feelings of envy, psychological distress including depression, anxiety, and instances of panic. The sentiments of insufficiency and diminished self-assurance that individuals with low self-esteem encounter can be surmounted through diligent effort exerted by oneself.

- When engaged in a romantic partnership, it is advised to record a minimum of one commendable characteristic relating to oneself within the context of the relationship on a daily basis. Irrespective of the events that unfold each day, ensure that you consistently engage in this singular task on a daily basis.

• Please proceed to apply the same approach to yourself when not considering the dynamics of the relationship. Allocate a few moments on two separate occasions during the day to express gratitude towards oneself for a personal attribute or accomplishment. Write this down.

• The majority of individuals typically encounter greater levels of acceptance rather than rejection, regardless of their subjective perceptions. Make a habit of observing regularly whether the individuals in your life display kindness or exhibit rejection. The most effective approach to address low self-esteem is to consistently expose oneself to a daily reality that embraces acceptance rather than rejection.

• Document all of these experiences in a journal and, at the conclusion of each week, convene a meeting with the individual you hold utmost trust in order to analyze the occurrences. Did you receive genuine support or encounter outright rejection?

• Having a constructive relationship provides a favorable benchmark in one's life. • The presence of a healthy relationship offers a beneficial frame of reference in one's life. • Being engaged in a positive relationship grants an advantageous point of comparison in one's life. To cultivate a more constructive relationship with oneself, it is advisable to strategically place affirmative notes in visible locations throughout one's home, ensuring frequent exposure and encouragement.

What is the Significance of Positive Thinking?

Optimistic thinking possesses immense potency and captivating allure. Ultimately, it bestows myriad advantages that merit careful consideration. It can facilitate the preservation of your desired lifestyle and guarantee the attainment of the success and happiness you aspire to in life. It will facilitate your transformation into the individual you have long aspired to be, guaranteeing your ability to effectively pursue and accomplish the objectives and aspirations close to your heart.

Consider this scenario: You aspire to acquire an academic qualification.

Nevertheless, the acquisition of such a degree will necessitate a significant investment of time, energy, and effort. While you may demonstrate an initial acceptance of this commitment, your persistent inability to face and overcome obstacles reveals a lack of perseverance. The absence of inherent resilience hinders your progress and ultimately leads to grave complications. Consequently, you perceive your failures as a direct result of encountering obstacles at various points throughout your journey. You think that you are failing because when you do try to make things work, something goes wrong, and that automatically means that you must be failing. Nevertheless, encountering occasional failures is customary and anticipated. However, the pervasive negativity persists and exerts a profound influence on every aspect of your being.

Ultimately, positive thinking effectively resolves that issue. It serves to remind you that you need not succumb to those adverse emotions. You need not allow yourself to be governed by that pessimistic storyline. "Optimism and constructive thinking will yield a plethora of advantages, which encompass:

Reduced likelihood of experiencing depression

Having a positive outlook significantly increases the likelihood of preventing the onset of depression.

Resistant to Stress

Positive thinkers do not encounter stress to the same extent as others. While it should not be implied that they never experience stress, it can be stated that they exhibit a remarkable ability to endure stress for considerably longer durations compared to individuals in their surroundings. They possess the capacity to refrain from succumbing to the overwhelming impact of negativity or stress in their lives, and this holds significant importance.

Happier

Typically, individuals who exhibit a positive mindset tend to uphold a more joyful way of life. It is customary for them to discern that it is considerably more probable for them to derive pleasure from their surroundings, as they possess the ability to contemplate matters without being burdened by pessimism.

Better Immune System

Research has, in fact, established a positive correlation between individuals possessing positive mindsets and the presence of stronger immune systems.

Maintaining a positive mindset and emotional state often contributes to bolstering the immune system, as opposed to having a weakened one. You will experience reduced susceptibility to illnesses and an increased probability of hastened recovery from common ailments such as the cold.

Better Wellbeing

One's overall well-being is typically enhanced by maintaining a positive mindset. Ultimately, positivity is purportedly associated with enhanced mindsets and improved lifestyles, both of which can subsequently be correlated with leading a more healthful existence.

Better Relationships

Studies have revealed that the cultivation of a positive mindset is imperative for the success and sustainability of marital relationships.

This should come as no astonishment—however, when taken on average, the optimal ratio is 5 to 1. Maintaining a ratio of five positive interactions to every negative one significantly increases the likelihood of leading a more fulfilling life and nurturing a healthier marital relationship. As the aforementioned ratio decreases, it becomes increasingly probable that the marriage will not endure.

Enhanced job success rates" "Superior job achievement rates" "Heightened job performance outcomes" "Improved job attainment metrics" "Optimized job success ratios

A positive mindset greatly increases the probability of achieving success in the professional realm. Your favorable work experiences are expected to yield significantly greater success compared to negative ones, on average. Notably, occupations that entail interpersonal engagements significantly derive advantages from incorporating positivity into such interactions.

Living Longer

Research indicates that individuals who cultivate a positive lifestyle experience a tangible increase in their life expectancy.

Enhanced Social Circle and Improved Social Interactions

Generally, individuals who exhibit a positive demeanor tend to cultivate a larger social circle, thereby contributing to an enhanced sense of happiness. Once you successfully sustain such an optimistic outlook and cultivate healthier connections with your loved ones, you shall observe a palpable increase in your overall happiness. The presence of positivity in your life will undoubtedly contribute to this uplifting effect.

Optimism Enhances Leadership Effectiveness

By maintaining a positive mindset, you can enhance your leadership abilities and thereby outperform your colleagues in terms of effectiveness and positive impact. Maintaining a positive perception among those around you is greatly enhanced when you are capable of consistently projecting a positive personal image. You will possess the capability to make decisions adeptly in high-pressure situations, exhibiting remarkable effectiveness. Additionally, you are more likely to garner the support of individuals in your vicinity.

Strategies for Cultivating a Positive Mindset

The act of maintaining a positive mindset bears resemblance to engaging in self-dialogue, albeit with some distinctions. Similar to self-talk, positive thinking refers to the energy, intention, and focal point we allocate to our internal dialogues. Presently, it is crucial to observe that maintaining a positive mindset is not inherently synonymous with experiencing perpetual happiness or constant joyfulness. In numerous instances throughout life, individuals may find it necessary or desirable to adopt a positive mindset despite experiencing distress, melancholy, or indifference within their emotions, internal sphere, or external circumstances. Possessing a 'constructive mental disposition' or practicing constructive cognition entails the capacity to adopt a positive and hopeful perspective toward any circumstance in one's life, with the aim of personal improvement, benefiting others, or positively influencing a particular situation or scenario. By implementing optimistic thinking in one's internal dialogue, a range of magnificent benefits can be experienced.

The convergence of an optimistic mindset with the narratives we weave about ourselves has the potential to enhance every facet of our existence. Positive self-talk has the potential to greatly improve various aspects of one's life, encompassing relationships of both an intimate and platonic nature, physical well-being, mental focus and clarity, cognitive abilities and attitude, enthusiasm and zest for life, and the willingness to pursue personal endeavors, aspirations, and goals. As elucidated in the introductory portion of this chapter, when individuals partake in self-dialogue, they effectively engage in an internal discourse. Given the intricate and interconnected nature of the self, along with its remarkable essence, adopting positive thinking and mental frameworks will prove highly advantageous.

How can we cultivate a positive mindset? As previously conveyed, maintaining a positive mindset extends beyond simplistic notions of optimism and idealism. Positive thinking entails acknowledging and embracing the inherent flaws or less desirable aspects of both oneself and life, and making a conscious decision to direct attention towards one's strengths. It is crucial to maintain awareness.

Selection is a highly crucial element in the process of reshaping and restructuring one's thoughts. By opting to adopt a positive mindset, we are effectively engaging in the process of reconfiguring, readjusting, and reshaping our cerebral structures, the intricate network of neurons, along with the cognitive thought processes and behavioral routines that impact our everyday existence. It is commonly understood that our thoughts possess a profound impact on all aspects of our lives - our mental state, physical well-being, and the world around us. Therefore, adjusting our viewpoints to those that are congruent and harmonious with a reality grounded in love, positivity, unity, connection, abundance, bliss, new prospects, and various other aspects related to a constructive and well-balanced state of mind significantly impacts the direction of our attention.

A suitable comparison would be to envision a spotlight. Envision the vast expanse of the cosmos, the celestial canopy, and the luminous celestial bodies during the nocturnal hours, and draw a parallel between this imagery and the realm of consciousness encompassing both the unconscious or subconscious mind, and the conscious mind, encompassing all forms of awareness and cognitive processes. Take a moment to envision directing a beam of light from a handheld illuminating device towards the expanse of the nocturnal heavens, with a clear and deliberate purpose of illuminating a singular celestial entity, be it a distant star, planet, or galaxy. The illumination serves as a manifestation of your intention and concentration.

You retain knowledge of the existence of other celestial bodies such as stars, planets, and galaxies; however, in that particular instance of focusing your light directly on a specific entity, your consciousness became finely attuned to it. Your consciousness underwent a shift, causing the cessation of all other celestial entities and the various aspects of universal awareness. Naturally, their presence persisted throughout, albeit the underlying notion lies in those instances of purposeful consciousness and deliberate concentration. It is during those moments wherein your entire energy and mental acuity were solely dedicated to the subject matter upon which you elected to illuminate. You deliberately illuminated something.

This is fundamentally the outcome that arises when we actively opt to partake in constructive thought patterns. The obscurity and all other facets of being persist and endure; it is solely our concentration that, with intentionality and awareness, notably influences whatever we direct our illumination towards. This serves as the intrinsic essence of adopting a positive mindset: It is apparent that both positive and negative aspects coexist, encompassing brightness and darkness; however, we perpetually retain the option to radiate illumination. Our cognitive abilities possess the capacity to illuminate.

Positive thinking can be attained through various approaches. These encompass neurolinguistics programming, meditation and mindfulness practices, the usage of mantras and affirmations, cognitive shaping techniques, specific forms of sound therapy like binaural beats, and engaging in self-hypnosis or positive self-talk.

Enhance Your Conflict Resolution Aptitude

Our collective desire is to effectively oversee and mitigate a situation, ideally avoiding any undesirable outcomes or, at the very least, minimizing any detrimental effects. But how many of us really can do that? How frequently have you interceded in a situation and achieved a mutually agreeable resolution?

Conflicts elicit intense emotional responses, which, if not properly addressed, can engender feelings of pain and disillusionment, potentially resulting in the breakdown of interpersonal relationships.

Conflicts are often a sign of healthy relationships. When individuals can articulate their perspectives to one another, even in the presence of disagreement, it illustrates the presence of an open relationship and mutual transparency between the parties involved. Nevertheless, it is within the context of conflicts that a multitude of adverse sentiments are evoked. During combat, one experiences heightened levels of anxiety, frustration, and apprehension. Due to the presence of intense emotions, there is an increased likelihood of engaging in irrational behavior that could potentially harm the relationship. In light of the circumstances, how do you effectively handle this intricate situation? In what manner do you and the other party/parties navigate this predicament while upholding the fundamental aspects of the relationship, while ensuring candor and integrity rather than resorting to mere politeness?

Consequently, what are the measures you take to enhance your aptitude in resolving conflicts?

Comprehend the nature of the conflict.

During the course of the conflict, it transcends mere dissension. A confrontation exerts physical strain to ensure vigilant readiness, even in the absence of an actual danger. To comprehend the conflict at hand, it is crucial to recognize that the other individual, much like yourself, experiences a sense of fear. Consequently, it is imperative to acknowledge that their concerns do not pertain to you.

Thus, it is imperative to invest time in discerning the root cause of the conflict. Were you at fault in this situation? If that is indeed the case, would you please offer a heartfelt apology? In the event that your partner was at fault, you could tactfully guide them towards acknowledging their mistake in a manner that is considerate and free from condescension.

Throughout this process, it is imperative to bear in mind that your conflict does not lie with the other individual, but rather stems from a particular matter. Therefore, refrain from making personal comments about the other individual and instead, consistently ensure that your remarks are related to the topic at hand. Instead of expressing "you are always hurting me," it would be more effective to phrase it as "whatever you say always causes me pain." This approach directs attention towards the impact of their words, rather than making a broad accusation against them.

Comprehend the requirements of the individual in question.

An additional aspect of conflict resolution entails consistently considering the perspective and needs of the other party involved. In the course of each exchange, endeavor to understand and appreciate their perspective. Every individual is entitled to receive respect and have their perspectives acknowledged. As a result, in order to effectively handle conflicts, it is crucial to consistently consider the inherent humanity of the other individual. It is imperative for us as humanity to assume the responsibility of comprehending our fellow beings - to recognize their emotions, desires, and perspectives. To gain insight into their perspectives and understand the underlying reasons behind their worldview, even in cases where our own beliefs may diverge.

Display a Willingness to Reach a Mutual Agreement

We universally experience the inclination to assert our correctness in a state of disagreement. Consequently, when the interlocutor expresses their viewpoint, you respond with your own perspective, ultimately leading to a situation where neither party truly comprehends one another during the discourse. This exchange of emotional expression is likely to foster feelings of animosity and exacerbate the deterioration of effective communication.

In order to enhance conflict management, it is imperative to attentively consider the perspective of the other party, while also ensuring that your viewpoint is heard, ultimately culminating in a mutually agreeable compromise that duly acknowledges the opinions of both individuals involved.

Engaging in compromise does not entail wavering on one's principles. On the contrary, it demonstrates your appreciation for the interpersonal connection and the requirements of the other individual.

Nevertheless, it is important to observe the circumstances in which you find yourself being the sole party making concessions or making the most substantial concessions following a dispute. This unilaterally imposed settlement exemplifies a manifestation of a dysfunctional partnership. Although it presents difficulties, achieving an equitable division of settlement can be facilitated by ensuring that neither party consistently bears an undue burden during conflicts.

When one places a high importance on winning an argument or asserting correctness, an unwillingness to actively listen to the other party arises, thereby exacerbating the breakdown in communication.

How To Handle Low Self-Esteem

A profound influence is exerted on individuals, particularly males, by a diminished sense of self-worth. In a society where men are conventionally regarded as the dominant gender, the assessment of one's self-worth can ultimately determine the outcome between achieving prosperity or experiencing disappointment. Each individual, irrespective of their gender, encounters personal challenges pertaining to self-assurance and self-esteem. For certain individuals, challenges related to confidence and self-esteem may be transitory hindrances; for others, they represent formidable obstacles to overcome.

Failing to effectively manage one's own personal perspective can lead to detrimental consequences in the long run. Minor setbacks that are left unaddressed have the potential to accumulate and transform into formidable challenges that will persistently plague you in the future. Insufficient self-confidence results in heightened stress levels, increased anxiety, susceptibility to depression, and feelings of solitude. In its utmost manifestation, it can render you susceptible to substance abuse and various deleterious conduct. It hinders scholastic and vocational achievement, and presents an obstacle to the establishment of substantial interpersonal connections.

Strategies for Enhancing Self-esteem Efficiency

Regardless of your negative self-perception, it is imperative to acknowledge that it has the potential for transformation. It is not inherently drastic; nonetheless, one's self-perception can certainly undergo a transformation, evolving from unfavorable to favorable, from negative to positive, and from pessimistic to optimistic. "Presented below are a selection of efficacious approaches to transform and improve one's self-perception:

Confront the Inner Self-Critic

It is imperative to bear in mind that self-esteem is intricately tied to one's individual perception of oneself. Should there indeed be an individual who holds highly critical views, it would be none other than yourself. There exists within you a facet that consistently asserts your fallibility. Address this detrimental aspect of your character and question your personal presuppositions. This critical self encompasses numerous aspects, and understanding the manner in which each facet presents itself will facilitate your ability to address them in a constructive manner.

The critic who displays unjustifiable and lacking in compassion qualities. This refers to your inner self that consistently directs its attention towards unfavorable aspects. Does the following strike a chord with you: "I am curious as to why my colleagues applauded during my presentation; I feel it may not have lived up to my personal expectations"? Alternatively, consider the following phrase: "In what manner could they have possibly failed to recognize the mistakes I made during that presentation?"

Rather than engaging in self-criticism and fixating on the negative aspects, adopt a new mindset that acknowledges room for improvement, such as: "It may not have been flawless, but I have identified areas where I can enhance my skills" or perhaps "I am pleasantly surprised by the positive reception my presentation has received." I am of the opinion that I performed well."

The unrealistic critic. This is the aspect of your personality that consistently sets high expectations for your performance, where deviating from perfection is perceived as a form of failure. This is the moment when one finds oneself uttering the thought, "It was merely a straightforward undertaking, so why am I unable to execute it accurately?" I'm just plain dumb!"

Instead of indulging in impracticality, analyze the experience by dissecting elements that were effective and those that were not. Value your accomplishments and strive to enhance your shortcomings. Perhaps one could express it as follows: "Despite potential shortcomings, I appreciate the effort I put into structuring and organizing the contents of this presentation." Perhaps I shall employ an alternative format on subsequent occasions."

The irrational critic. You are making hasty generalizations based on superficial observations. Oh, it appears that she is not directing her gaze towards me. She has expressed her reluctance to engage in conversation with me. I'm really a loser."

Rather than engaging in irrationality and drawing your own conclusion, it would be advisable to directly address your perceived reality. Indeed, she appears to be actively evading me, although I remain uncertain as to the reason behind such behavior. "I will simply engage her and inquire." Confronting your perception directly elevates you from indulging in self-pity and unjustified despondency. Do not be overly concerned should your perception happen to be correct, as it presents you with the chance to address any areas for improvement, rather than hastily condemning oneself as a total failure.

The doomsday critic. Presently, you exhibit characteristics that reflect your lowest state, assuming the role of a harbinger of misfortune, perceiving minor errors as catastrophic events. Regrettably, my application has been declined. I shall perpetually lack the merit necessary to attain anything of value. Nobody will hire me."

Cease! Exercise pragmatism and acknowledge that this is merely one unsuccessful endeavor. Although being rejected can cause pain, it is important to understand that it does not define your worth as a person.

Be Compassionate—to Yourself!

Instead of engaging in self-criticism, endeavor to exhibit greater self-compassion. You possess the ability to demonstrate benevolence and understanding towards your acquaintances; it is fitting to extend the same treatment towards yourself. Your analytical self expresses disapproval towards another aspect of your character. As you encounter your inner critic, it is equally important to cultivate a sense of empathy towards all facets of your complete character. This holds utmost significance when confronted with challenging circumstances; this is when it becomes imperative to support oneself. Allow me to present several instances of demonstrating self-compassion:

Be the pioneer in displaying forgiveness towards missed opportunities. The occurrence of events in this world is not always aligned with your designated plan. Acknowledging this truth will facilitate your acceptance of the notion that you are not exempt from error. Rather than expressing criticism, engage in self-soothing by offering affirmations and encouragement, reassuring yourself that things will ultimately work out positively.

Respect your being human. We are all susceptible to making errors; it is inherent in our human nature. Acknowledging your inherent fallibility entails recognizing that there exist instances in which you may not exhibit optimal performance. Rather than chastising oneself for the error, one should strive to learn from it and enhance oneself.

Acquire the aptitude to regulate your emotions, rather than allowing them to take control. Feelings obscure our interpretation of the surrounding environment, particularly those of a pessimistic nature. While acknowledging one's emotions is crucial, it is of utmost importance to ensure that these sentiments are not allowed to overpower one's rationality. In the event of experiencing feelings of sadness, isolation, or disheartenment, it is advisable to document the individual consequences of these emotions on a personal level. After overcoming one's emotional state, it is advisable to retrospectively evaluate one's written thoughts, as the process often reveals a surprising disparity in perception when emotions do not exert dominance over one's cognition.

Disassemble the barricade of your seclusion

Individuals with diminished self-regard tend to engage in self-imposed seclusion as they perceive themselves as undeserving of assistance or recognition. It is imperative to dismantle the barriers you have constructed around yourself in order to foster the growth of your self-esteem. Your self-perception has extensively governed your life; it is now opportune to grant other individuals the ability to offer an alternative perspective on your character. Notwithstanding the challenges, you can always rely on the support of individuals in your vicinity who are inclined to assist.

Engage in a candid and sincere discussion with your acquaintances. Undoubtedly, there exists an individual with whom you experience a sense of intimacy and ease. Please ensure that you are transparent about your emotions and clearly communicate the assistance you require from your closest companions. On occasion, your acquaintances possess a more comprehensive understanding of your predicament than you yourself may possess. To what extent have your acquaintances offered you solace and reassurance during periods of emotional distress? This is the appropriate moment to attentively hear what they have to say.

The proverbial wisdom "like-minded individuals congregate together" will not be applicable to your circumstances. Avoid associating with individuals who will only engage in commiseration and succumb to feelings of self-pity and depression. You are not exhibiting selfishness in this scenario; rather, you simply require the presence of individuals who can encourage your personal growth and development.

Contact individuals in positions of power within your sphere. If you are a student, it is advisable to engage in conversation with your professor, guidance counselor, advisor, or coach. These individuals possess a wealth of expertise in addressing the personality issues faced by their students, accumulated over several years of experience. If you are an employee, engage in dialogue with your co-workers or your superiors. Engage in a conversation with your colleagues regarding the obstacles you have encountered in your professional environment, elucidating that you require their assistance in order to overcome your reservations and achieve personal growth. You will be astounded by the response you will receive if you approach individuals for aid. Certain individuals are simply awaiting your initiative to establish contact with them.

Talk to a professional. It is imperative to consult experienced psychologists or therapists if the underlying source of your diminished self-esteem stems from significant past encounters. There is no fault in seeking assistance from trained professionals.

Alter your cognitive frameworks
A peculiar aspect pertaining to individuals' discernment of actuality is that, quite often, their perception of

reality is merely an outcome of their cognitive routines. If one consistently tends to interpret things in the most negative manner imaginable, it becomes quite effortless to arrive at the conclusion that this is the sole manner in which individuals can elucidate these signals. This is the only form of justice available to them. Considering that one tends to perceive reality based on preconceived notions arising from specific feedback or stimuli, it can be inferred that the assumed perception aligns with actuality. Well, your inclination towards thinking in that manner could be attributed to your accustomed thinking patterns. Your cognitive processes are structured in a manner that consistently leads to a specific inference.

What if you were to alter your cognitive patterns? What if you were to alter your cognitive processes? Does it inevitably entail that you would arrive at identical assessments? It is highly probable that one's perception of self-worth and personal value may undergo a transformation upon the alteration of one's mental patterns.

Consequently, it is imperative to acknowledge the fundamental piece of information that mental habits are consciously selected. I understand that this assertion may appear implausible, as one might contemplate, "I simply came into existence with these innate attributes." This is simply my sentiment. You might want to reconsider your perspective, as the manner in which you interpret your reality must have originated from a source. It is a skill or knowledge that you acquired through personal experience or education. The majority of individuals acquire their cognitive patterns from their parents. We also acquire this knowledge through consistent association with individuals in our social circles. The phenomenon known as groupthink does indeed exist. Should you alter your social circle, you may be astounded by the subsequent transformations in your cognitive patterns and demeanor.

Nevertheless, it is imperative that you scrutinize your cognitive patterns. It is a matter of personal choice. It is not an innate trait. It does not constitute an imposition beyond your control, leaving you devoid of options. You consistently possess the capacity for making choices. One can continue to remain aware of their mental habits and actively resist them.

A Practice In Positive Thinking

I would appreciate if you could endeavor to compile a list. Individuals who hold a pessimistic view of their capabilities may encounter difficulties in this task. However, it is important to note that it is achievable for all individuals. Thus, it is advised to exhibit patience and self-compassion throughout the process. The inventory shall encompass all the elements that instill joy and satisfaction into your life. These will entail tasks within your repertoire, which you possess knowledge of and are at ease accomplishing. Should you encounter any challenges with this, I recommend briefly closing your eyes and reflecting upon moments in your life that evoked a sense of joy. By conducting a thorough analysis, one can discern the specific actions undertaken that elicited feelings of happiness and confidence. As an illustrative example, you might recall a specific event in which you experienced a profound sense of self-satisfaction and contentment. It is of no consequence as to who or what caused the disruption. Please make an effort to recollect that sensation and compile a record of the factors that evoked a sense of unparalleled triumph.

We shall not devote our attention to the negative aspects of self-perception that have consumed you for an excessive duration. Presently, you are at a critical juncture in your life where it is crucial to possess a compilation of positive aspects to reflect upon whenever an individual or circumstance manages to undermine your self-worth. I recollect a specific occurrence during my adolescence wherein I donned an exceptional ensemble and received admiration for my appearance. Certainly, I can accomplish that presently; however, it is often observed that individuals harboring pessimism and low self-regard tend to overlook the instances in their lives when they truly excelled, as every individual undoubtedly possesses such moments. Irrespective of the simplicity of one's thoughts, they should be diligently recorded due to their inherent significance to one's existence.

A demonstration of one's own self-assuredness

Within this exercise, I encourage you to direct your attention towards your bodily alignment. Observe your reflection in the mirror and, if available, position a full-length mirror in a manner where you can perceive your own entry into a room. Insufficient self-assurance is apparent in one's gait and demeanor when interacting with the external environment. There appears to be a pronounced inclination of your head. It appears that your shoulders exhibit a slight drooping inclination, and there is a tendency for your hands to become restless in response to interpersonal communication. Today, I kindly request that you rectify your posture. You should ensure that your gaze remains fixed forward. It is imperative that you maintain proper posture with your shoulders held in an upright position. If you have developed a habit of slouching, it is crucial to be exceedingly aware that this detrimental posture diminishes your stature. Your countenance additionally reveals your true emotions. If one is unable to make direct eye contact and present a pleasant expression, it may project an image of lack of self-assurance and hint at potential personal challenges. Engage in mirror practice and subsequently stroll down the street while adopting the recommended posture, accompanied by courteous smiles directed towards individuals encountered along the way.

Self-assurance is also evident in the manner in which you articulate yourself. Certain individuals may experience difficulty communicating with others. Therefore, I kindly request that you capture your voice as a means of addressing this matter. Perform this activity within the confines of your personal residence, specifically in the seclusion of your chamber, where you may acquaint yourself with others beforehand, and subsequently appraise the audible rendition of your own voice.

Individuals often acquire rather indolent tendencies and may exhibit a lack of enunciation in their speech. Let\'s try it again. On this occasion, please assume the role of a renowned actor and proceed to formally reintroduce yourself. By assuming an additional role, you are effectively equipping yourself to communicate in the manner expected of the actor. Now make another attempt, envisioning a scenario where you are communicating with your supervisor, assuming an equal level of significance. Individuals with a deficiency in self-assurance oftentimes exhibit submissiveness, a trait that frequently leads them into various predicaments. Envision yourself as an instructor engaged in imparting knowledge on the rudiments of the alphabet to a group of students. Please record the lesson once more, keeping in mind that you are working with children who experience challenges in the learning process. You must articulate your words with utmost clarity to eliminate any possible ambiguity in your message. Practice it again. Continue to repeat the process until you achieve a state of contentment and willingness to acknowledge the sound emitted when you engage in playback of the recording.

Before we finish with the recording, I want you to record these sentences and mean it, because you will use this as a reminder to yourself that you are every bit as important as anyone else.

I am an individual of substantial value, deserving of one's acquaintance. I am approachable and sociable, and I have no aversion to interacting with individuals."

Now, moving forward to the subsequent section of the exercise, I would like to assess your capability to provide selflessly without any expectation of reciprocation. Needy individuals or individuals with diminished self-esteem tend to disproportionately seek excessive approval. One may desire the confirmation of their superior to validate their competence, distinguishing themselves from their colleagues who may be content with solely fulfilling their duties. Continuously seeking validation from others diminishes the likelihood of receiving a promotion. It is evident that your lack of self-assurance necessitates seeking validation from others, which can have adverse effects on those in your proximity as individuals who depend on constant affirmation can be burdensome. In the pursuit of life's endeavors, it is imperative that one develops the capacity to engage in them for personal fulfillment rather than for the sake of appeasing others. The opinions of others hold little weight as long as you find satisfaction in your own actions. The elation and self-assurance derived from fostering expectations devoid of any potential rewards is truly remarkable. Please select a task that you are capable of undertaking for a friend or a neighbor. You may consider preparing a cake for an elderly resident in your neighborhood or offering your assistance by taking dogs on walks at the nearby animal shelter as potential activities to engage in. I kindly request your assistance in this matter, as it is crucial to recognize that the only individual who truly needs to be aware of your benevolent actions is yourself. Please complete the task without anticipating any outcomes. Don\'t expect praise. Don't boast about what you did.

Indulge in this pursuit solely driven by your desire for inner satisfaction, and undoubtedly, the anticipated outcome shall be realized.

The objective of these exercises is to endeavor towards enhancing one's perception and perception of oneself. Engaging in volunteering can assist you in achieving that objective, however, it is essential not to engage in volunteer activities with the sole intention of seeking recognition or attention. This introduces a sense of necessity into the scenario, and your current requirement is solely to derive personal satisfaction from your actions.

www.ingramcontent.com/pod-product-compliance
Lightning Source LLC
Chambersburg PA
CBHW050233120526
44590CB00016B/2070